MOTOCROSS

BY JOHN HAMILTON

A&D Xtreme
An imprint of Abdo Publishing | www.abdopublishing.com

Visit us at
www.abdopublishing.com

Published by Abdo Publishing Company, a division of ABDO, PO Box 398166, Minneapolis, Minnesota 55439. Copyright ©2015 by Abdo Consulting Group, Inc. International copyrights reserved in all countries. No part of this book may be reproduced in any form without written permission from the publisher. A&D Xtreme™ is a trademark and logo of Abdo Publishing Company.

Printed in the United States of America, North Mankato, Minnesota.
042014
092014

Editor: Sue Hamilton
Graphic Design: John Hamilton
Cover Photo: Thinkstock
Interior Photos: Corbis, pg. 4-5, 6, 7, 8-9, 10-11, 16, 17 (upper right) 18-19, 20, 21, 22, 23, 24-25, 26, 26-27, 28, 29, 32; Thinkstock, pg. 1, 2-3, 12-13, 14, 15, 17 (chest protector, boots), 30-31.

Websites
To learn more about Action Sports, visit booklinks.abdopublishing.com. These links are routinely monitored and updated to provide the most current information available.

Library of Congress Control Number: 2014932223

Cataloging-in-Publication Data

Hamilton, John.
  Motocross / John Hamilton.
    p. cm. -- (Action sports)
Includes index.
ISBN 978-1-62403-442-8
1. Motocross--Juvenile literature.   I. Title.
796.7/56--dc23

2014932223

CONTENTS

DOWN IN THE DIRT

Motocross combines motorcycle racing with the adrenaline-pumping thrill of riding dirt bikes. It is a popular motor sport worldwide. Outdoor tracks can be tightly packed down or they can be muddy messes.

Competitors race around sharp corners. They get big air over jumps. They fight to cross the finish line in first place.

Xtreme Fact: *Motocross is a combination of the French word* motocyclette *and the phrase* "cross country."

HISTORY

Motocross got its start from motorcycle competitions held in the United Kingdom in the early 1900s. Races were called scrambles. By the 1950s, dirt bikes were invented that were very tough. They could handle bumpy tracks and hard landings. Motocross exploded in popularity in the United States in the 1980s.

Young motocross riders in 1975.

An English motocross scramble held in 1952. The competitor, B.G. Stonebridge, is riding a 498 Matchless bike.

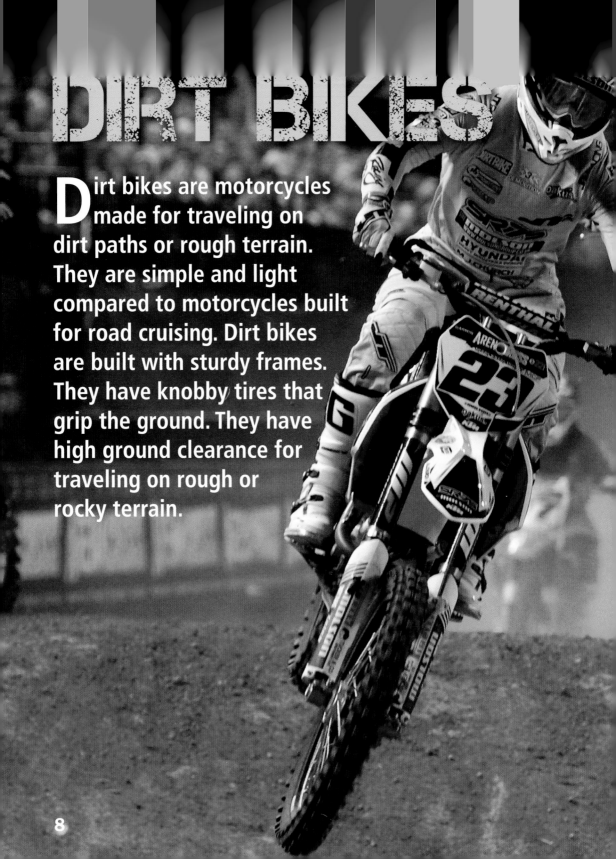

DIRT BIKES

Dirt bikes are motorcycles made for traveling on dirt paths or rough terrain. They are simple and light compared to motorcycles built for road cruising. Dirt bikes are built with sturdy frames. They have knobby tires that grip the ground. They have high ground clearance for traveling on rough or rocky terrain.

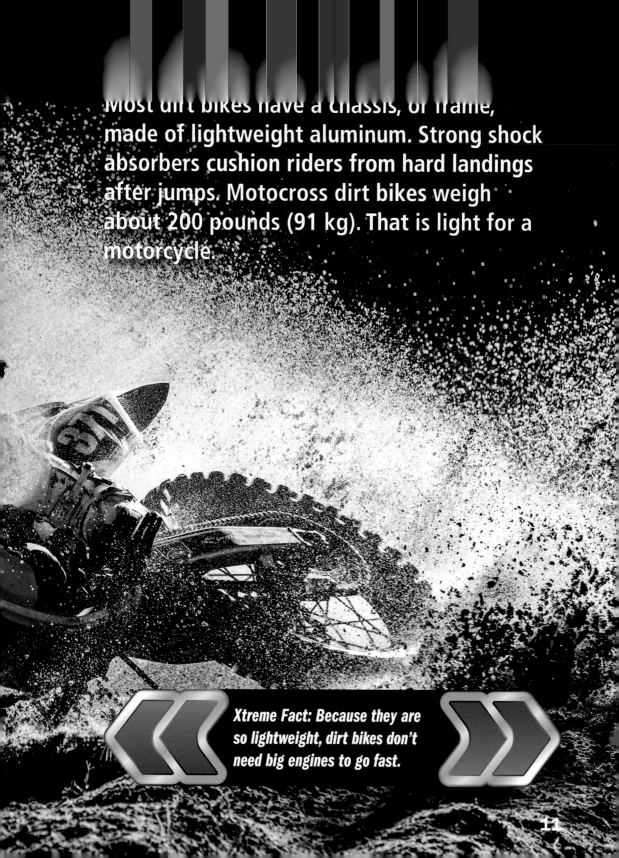

Most dirt bikes have a chassis, or frame, made of lightweight aluminum. Strong shock absorbers cushion riders from hard landings after jumps. Motocross dirt bikes weigh about 200 pounds (91 kg). That is light for a motorcycle.

Xtreme Fact: Because they are so lightweight, dirt bikes don't need big engines to go fast.

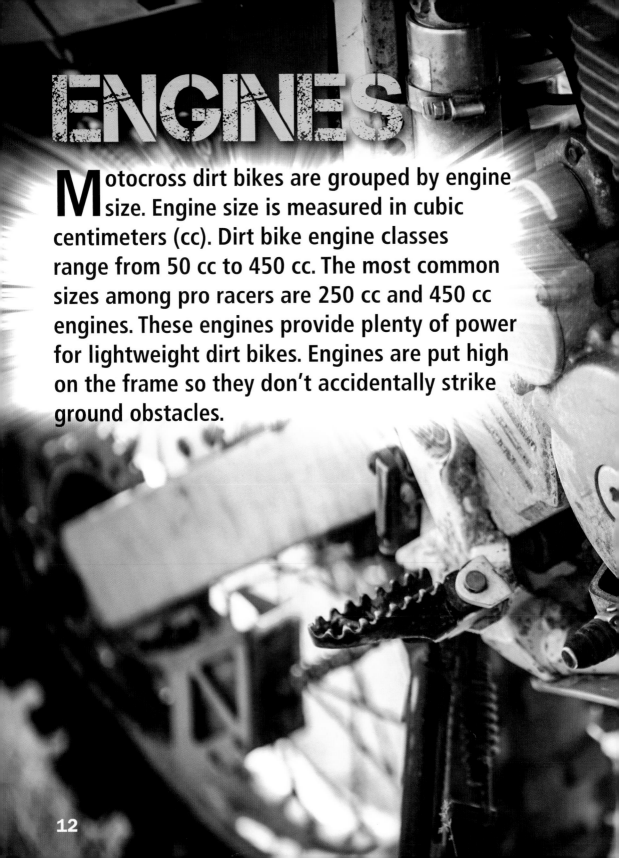

ENGINES

Motocross dirt bikes are grouped by engine size. Engine size is measured in cubic centimeters (cc). Dirt bike engine classes range from 50 cc to 450 cc. The most common sizes among pro racers are 250 cc and 450 cc engines. These engines provide plenty of power for lightweight dirt bikes. Engines are put high on the frame so they don't accidentally strike ground obstacles.

Xtreme Fact: Dirt bike engines have large air filters. They keep dust and dirt from clogging the engines.

TIRES

Dirt bike tires have deep treads for gripping loose dirt or muddy roads. The extra traction is important for motocross racing. These tires are called "nobbies."

Xtreme Fact: The raised rubber knobs dig into the ground, helped by the weight of the bike. This provides maximum traction.

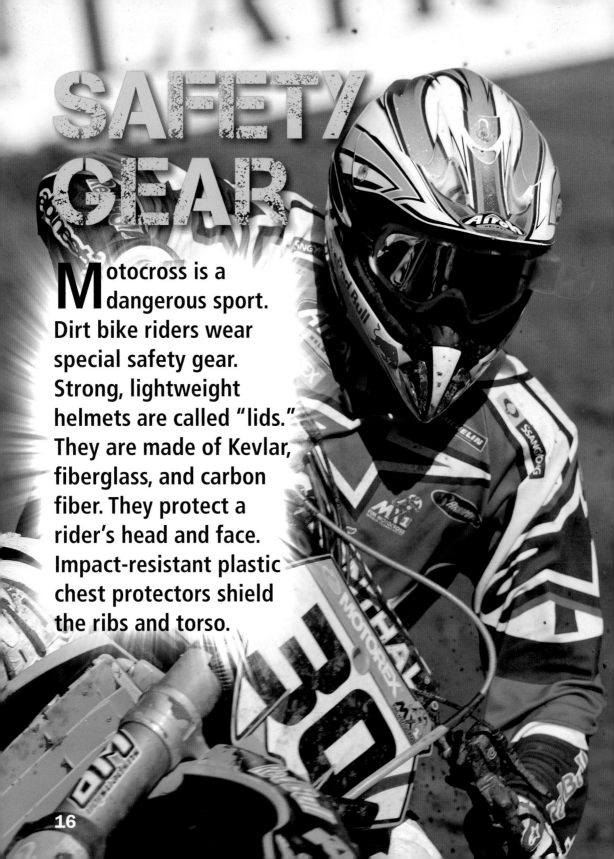

SAFETY GEAR

Motocross is a dangerous sport. Dirt bike riders wear special safety gear. Strong, lightweight helmets are called "lids." They are made of Kevlar, fiberglass, and carbon fiber. They protect a rider's head and face. Impact-resistant plastic chest protectors shield the ribs and torso.

Shirts, pants, and gloves are padded and breathable. They are flexible enough to give riders plenty of freedom. Tough leather boots are reinforced with plastic shields that protect a motocross rider's calves and shins.

Chest protector

Boots

MOTOCROSS RACING

Motocross racing is also called MX. Races are usually held on outdoor off-road tracks. The tracks are short. They range in length from .5 to 2 miles (.8 to 3.2 km).

Xtreme Fact: Motocross tracks include challenging obstacles, such as sharp turns, earthen berms, and jumps.

The best professional racers compete in the Lucas Oil Pro Motocross Championship. It is sanctioned by AMA Pro Racing. It is a 12-round series of races held across the United States.

Ryan Villopoto clears a jump in the Lucas Oil Pro Motocross Championship, AMA National held at Muddy Creek Raceway in Blountville, Tennessee.

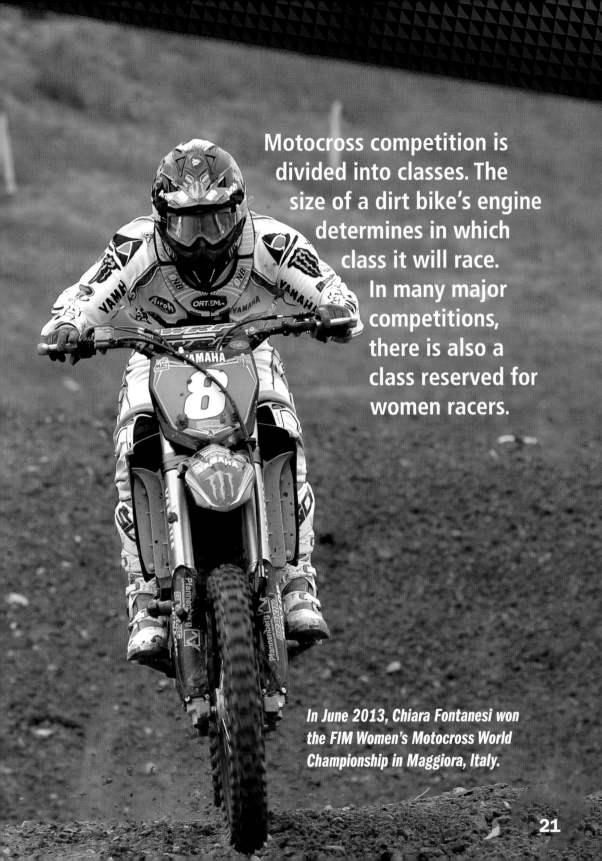

Motocross competition is divided into classes. The size of a dirt bike's engine determines in which class it will race. In many major competitions, there is also a class reserved for women racers.

In June 2013, Chiara Fontanesi won the FIM Women's Motocross World Championship in Maggiora, Italy.

After qualifying for a race, up to 40 competitors line up at a metal starting gate.

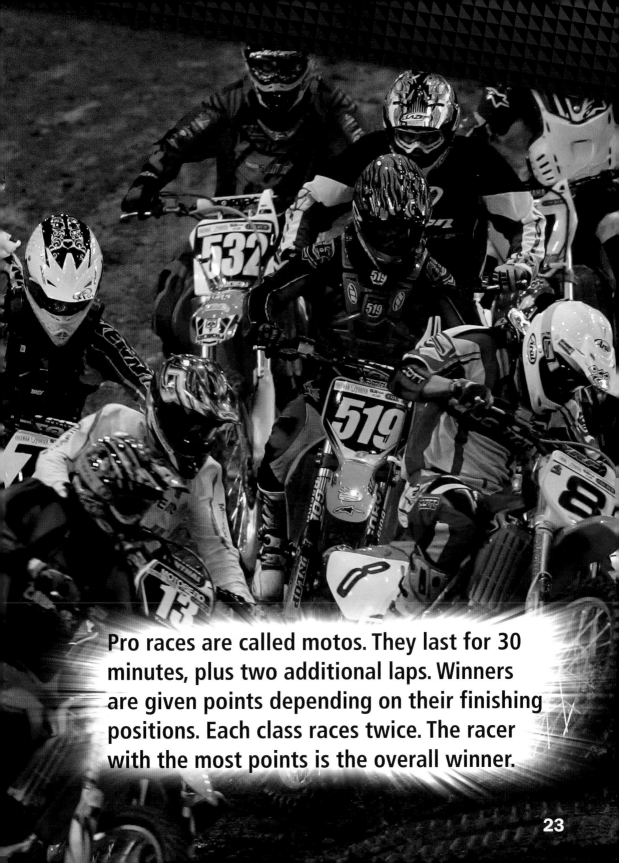

Pro races are called motos. They last for 30 minutes, plus two additional laps. Winners are given points depending on their finishing positions. Each class races twice. The racer with the most points is the overall winner.

SUPERCROSS

Supercross is a motor sport that grew out of motocross. Tracks are usually built in large indoor stadiums, with man-made dirt tracks. Supercross jumps and obstacles are more challenging. Turns are tighter and straightaways are shorter.

Xtreme Fact: The professional Supercross season is usually held in the winter and spring months.

ATV MOTOCROSS

A relatively new event is ATV/quad motocross (also called ATVMX). The ATV National Motocross Championship series was started in 1985. Competitors race on four-wheeled all-terrain vehicles (ATVs). Like regular motocross, ATV motocross races are held on outdoor dirt tracks, with challenging turns and jumps.

Many races feature mud bogs.

FREESTYLE MOTOCROSS

Freestyle motocross is also called FMX. Instead of racing, competitors try to get high scores by performing daredevil midair stunts. These death-defying tricks have colorful names such as the Hart Attack, the Nac Nac, and the Kiss of Death.

Backflip

Double-Grab Hart Attack

Completing a Double-Footed Nac Nac

Judges score each rider based on difficulty and style. Freestyle motocross gained popularity in the mid-1990s during ESPN's X Games competition.

Kiss of Death

GLOSSARY

CC (Cubic Centimeters)

Engines are often compared by measuring the amount of space (displacement) inside the cylinders where gas and air mix and are ignited to produce power. Displacement is measured in cubic centimeters.

Hart Attack

Named after Carey Hart, the first rider to popularize the trick (which is why the trick is called a "Hart" attack, not a "heart" attack). With both legs pointed straight up, one hand grabs the seat while the other remains on the handlebar.

Kevlar

A light and very strong man-made fiber. It is used to make helmets, vests, and other protective gear for sports, military, and law enforcement personnel.

Kiss of Death

A freestyle motocross trick in which the rider flips the bike into a near-vertical position, then performs a handstand while gripping the handlebars.

Nac Nac

A trick in which the rider throws one leg over the back of the bike to the other side, as if he or she is dismounting. In a double-footed nac nac, also called a nine-o'clock nac nac, the rider throws both feet in the air.

Traction

The grip of a vehicle's tires on the road or ground.

X Games

Extreme sporting events, such as motocross competitions, that are broadcast each year in the summer and winter by the ESPN television network.

INDEX